Spooky Success: An to the Law of Ir

by John Gold

Copyright © 2014 John Gold

The right of John Gold to be identified as the author of this work has been asserted in accordance with Section 77 of the Copyright, Designs and Patents Act 1988.

All rights reserved. No part of this publication may be reproduced, stored in a retrieval system, or transmitted, in any form or by any means, electronic, mechanical, photocopying, recording or otherwise, without the prior permission of the publisher.

The author of this book is a facilitator of general advice to help uncover your potential. The content of this book is therefore intended to be educational only. No content should be interpreted as advocating any form of business strategy or investment advice. Similarly, no content should be interpreted as offering any form of physical or mental health advice, or any kind of treatment whatsoever for emotional or medical problems. Always seek the advice and counsel of appropriately qualified business and medical professionals. The author assumes no responsibility for your actions, directly or indirectly, in reading the contents of this work.

Acknowledgement

To Anne McGhee, who passed into the next room but left the lights on for us.

Table of Contents

Chapter 1: An Introduction to Spooky Success   5-15

Chapter 2: Interactions from Non-Physical Levels   16-24

Chapter 3: The Universal Fabric and You   25-37

Chapter 4: Socialization and Your Escape Velocity   38-48

Chapter 5: From Positive Ripples to Positive Waves 49-54

Chapter 6: In Summary - The Quickie Action Plan   55-58

Chapter 7: Finally, Some Wise Words from an Old Bear 59-63

Chapter 1

An Introduction to Spooky Success

So, everything happens for a reason? You've heard that before. Perhaps you're skeptical, but for some reason you currently find yourself reading this short book — written by someone whom you've never met and who is perhaps thousands of miles away. Well, it's not really a surprise that you're reading this. It's part of your journey. In the past you weren't quite ready to read this; yet, now here it is, like an impish little friend who is sitting on your shoulder and asking: 'Well...?'

We meet at an intersection in space and time: an intersection that is not random or barren. In contrast, it is fused with kinetic energy. In a sense, today really is the first day of the rest of your life.

You see, let's put things into perspective. You're a unique entity and more powerful than you can possibly imagine. Formed from the dust of supernovas that exploded billions of years ago and billions of miles away, you're a work of indescribable evolutionary engineering. You're also part of a great fabric — an interconnected social web of the visible and invisible that creates worlds. Billions of connective events within that fabric ultimately combined to create you and to lead you here. So, welcome. As you inhabit a small ball of rock spinning at thousands of miles per hour through space around a large fireball, it would be sufficient to step back and wonder: 'Wow!'

Wow moments are usually wrapped up in the camouflage of our day-to-day reality. What appears to be routine is often anything but. For example, today someone was born who will shape your world in some way. Perhaps they'll invent something that you'll use. Perhaps they'll become a president or perhaps they'll just shake down a dusty old rug and the ripple effect will eventually reach you weeks later through weather patterns.

As well as interacting with our colleagues in the physical domain, mankind has always gazed up in wonder and sought the approval of 'the Gods', fate, or providence. Instinctively, most of us feel a part of something much bigger and more powerful. For millennia, runes have been examined, fortune tellers have been consulted and prayers have been said. Signs have also been sought and interpreted, and a higher state of consciousness has been the target destination for many in the arts and those on spiritual journeys.

Spooky power is nothing new. It's as old as human civilisation. An innate belief in the supercharged abilities of the paranormal has been a constant thread from the Stone Age to the Electronic Age. While the ancients engaged in the cult of Dionysus to seek that higher state, modern society interacts with self-help books, narcotics, organized religion and a myriad of commercial metaphysical products. Spooky power has been credited with saving lives, triggering new inventions and helping to produce some of the best artistic works known to man. On the downside, its dark side has sometimes been blamed for the worst forms of human behavior (look up the Nazis and the occult, for example).

Perhaps you don't need to go looking for spooky power. Perhaps it's already in the room with you and you only need to tune into it. After all, interconnectedness is the engine of life — whether seen or unseen. It is the dynamic that pushes us forward and you are a key part of that dynamic. You are the product of billions of interactions that took place over billions of years – any one of which would have meant that you wouldn't be around or reading this book; so everything is miraculous when you really pause and think about it.

Some interactions are obvious; others less so. Your life has been shaped by a number of interactions that have taken place in the so called supernatural world. Indeed, the metaphysical domain is all around us. Consider the influence of religion and the number of churches, mosques and synagogues that are peppered around our cities, towns and villages in cognizance of this influence: whether or not you believe in the tales of mankind interacting with spirits, angels, saints and a host of other non-physical entities, it is clear that they have had a practical bearing on the fabric of today's modern societies.

Between the 15th and 19th centuries, the Spanish, British and French went forth around the globe with the underlying value systems of Christianity — based on a compilation of books that were hallmarked by supernatural tales. When they created the Hispano-sphere (the Spanish-speaking world), the Anglo-sphere (the English-speaking world) and the Franco-sphere (the French-speaking world) they took these supernatural stories along with them and helped mould many of the societies that we know and recognize today.

The narrative momentum of the Bible was one of the supernatural and natural worlds continuously interconnecting and shaping destinies — sometimes of individuals, sometimes of whole nations. I'm here to remind you that such interactions did not stop when we entered the modern era.

Even to this day, the Vatican City, a sovereign state, will only canonize an individual – and in doing so recognize them for sainthood – after they firmly believe them to have been directly involved in two miraculous interventions (usually cures for the terminally ill). Such supernatural success stories are not shunned or considered to be 'spooky'; instead they are lauded. Indeed, whenever a new saint is identified, they are cheered in elaborate ceremonies by tens of thousands of well-wishers in broad daylight in St. Peter's Square.

Isn't it a little ironic that the Vatican is also a Permanent Observer at the United Nations — that grand New York edifice of international bureaucracy and endless committees? There, the men in suits and the men in clerical collars mingle together in the same corridors, discuss the same issues and consider the same solutions to our day-to-day problems.

No one calls sainthood 'spooky success.' You don't need to be a religious person, to recognize that powerful forces abound beyond our immediate perceptions. They are all around us. Successful people often remark on moments of inspiration, weird coincidences that took place and events that were downright spooky: as if the forces of nature – mighty, powerful, primeval forces – decided to get behind them at exactly the right time and propel them to achievements beyond their wildest dreams.

We've always been intrigued by stories of magical objects such as the genie in the lamp, and we've all heard about powerful historical objects and artefacts such as the Ark of the Covenant. Indeed, personal lucky charms are still commonplace in our supposedly rational and secular society. A belief in such superstitions hints at a common underlying awareness of the potential influence of the supernatural, and a shaping of real world events through the unseen mechanics of good or bad energy patterns within the non-physical world. Perhaps these items and trinkets just make us feel good and, in reality, we are actually surrounded at all times by energy patterns that are beyond our immediate perceptions.

Do interactions in other dimensions also have an impact upon our own dimensions and day-to-day experience? I believe the answer is yes, but you'll probably only notice them if you want to. If you follow a religion, then you will already have faith in the veracity of these interactions. Think of how major religions such as Christianity, Judaism and Islam are all rooted in interaction — and sometimes direct dialogue — between the physical and the non-physical. If you follow these belief systems, and billions do, then you'll earnestly hold the view that God communicated directly, or through angelic representatives, with Abraham, Moses, and Jesus; or that the Archangel Gabriel visited the Prophet Muhammad in the Cave of Hira, near Mecca.

Books also abound, for example, about personal guardian angels and how they will 'keep an eye' on you — for a while anyway — as we must remember that all that is physical must ultimately dissolve and reform (even suns, planets and whole galaxies have a shelf-life, so don't be too upset that us bags of water and minerals have natural shelf-lives too; again, it's designed that way).

Can you also tap into these unseen forces and energies? Can you harness them? Are they on your side?

Our understanding of physical nature is only beginning to be filled in — this is manifest in fairly recent scientific research into all-pervasive dark energy and dark matter. In contrast, with a few exceptions, research into the metaphysical is usually shunned by Establishment science, precisely because it is considered to fall outside the boundaries of the physical domain and is therefore viewed as being beyond our understanding.

Despite such conventional wisdom, something has led you to this book. Was it merely a coincidence? I don't think so. Of the millions of printed materials out there, we've connected at this point in time. You're perhaps here because you're unhappy or unfulfilled about something in your life. Maybe you feel that you've underachieved or have a general gut feeling that there's something missing at the moment. And you know something? You're probably correct. Most of us do underachieve in a material or social sense and are right to feel unfulfilled.

I suspect that our meeting is not taking place within a vacuum and that you are already more spiritually aware than the average person. We are the product of our life experiences. A first year Sociology student would confirm that. Perhaps you can sense a greater awareness of the spiritual enlightenment that is taking place around the world. Perhaps you have also witnessed irregular, unexplained, or spooky events in your lifetime. These may have made you wonder about the origin and intentions of such forces; after all, as the physicists tell us, energy cannot be created or destroyed, only transformed. Like a power station, can you tap into these forces and powers that, on closer analysis, appear to be bountiful throughout our planet and beyond?

Man has an internal engine, an internal compass and an internal sense of destiny, and somewhere down the line, as if on the dashboard of a car, your engine has signalled a little red light. Like fog gradually clearing up on a winter's morning, your false consciousness is lifting and you're probably now aware of some kind of gap in where you are, compared to where you want to be.

Trust your instincts to bridge that gap. Yes, like many other people, you could sit in the front of the TV digesting soap operas and sports forever, but that little voice in your head is saying: 'Raise your antenna because you might pick up something.'

Like spooky static coming through a radio, here I am. I'm not a genie in a bottle, but I'm here to give you a little nudge along the way. Through serendipity, I've entered your life with good intentions. Like you, I'd also like to see a better world and I'd also like you to perform like the high-speed dream machine that you could be; instead of being locked away in a proverbial garage covered up in a dusty tarpaulin with the occasional spider for company.

This short book is a starting gun for the next chapter of your life. Size really isn't important when it comes to the written word, so I am keeping this introductory work fairly brief and digestible as I would prefer you to be engaged in action-orientation.

Let's face it … the Law of Attraction doesn't work for some people … and whenever this occurs there's that catch-all reason often thrown back: you must have self-sabotaged somewhere along the line.

In this book, a different and compelling perspective – the Law of Interaction – examines your place within the physical and non-physical dimensions. This law is omnipresent. It is also powerful. It is a part of your daily life. It can inspire you, but it can also cause blockages and deprive you of your true destiny.

Note that in the realm of personal growth and self-improvement, the Law of Interaction has nothing to do with Sir Isaac Newton (1643-1727) and his 3rd Law of Motion – we'll leave that to more traditionally-minded people in white coats in Physics labs. Here, the Law of Interaction considers how you relate socially to a world that is interconnected physically, but also – and here is the key part – on an unseen, non-physical level too.

Spooky success through the Law of Interaction is introduced to you as a social dynamic and not a law of Physics. Where the Law of

Attraction focuses on your inner Psychology, the Law of Interaction recognizes that you are part of a much greater interconnected fabric and therefore incorporates aspects of the discipline of Sociology.

I would like to make the following very clear from the outset: the Law of Interaction is not part of mainstream Sociology; so this is unconventional material that requires an open mind and an ability to move beyond orthodoxy (although Parasociology is a nascent branch of this social science and I salute those who are taking the embryonic steps to develop this).

However, some of the basic concepts discussed here such as socialization and symbolic interactionism are indeed taught in schools, colleges and universities every day across the world.

In a nutshell, the Law of Interaction dictates that you are the product of your life experiences – this includes your environment and the other 'actors' with whom you interact on a daily basis. We are shaped and moulded by these significant others and by embedded circumstances – and herein lies a key artificial barrier to your growth strategy.

In a world that is also influenced by non-physical entities and unseen forces, the Law of Interaction must also account for those influences.

No one ever achieved success entirely on their own, and you will be no different to that. Due to the process of continual interaction between the physical and non-physical, 'spooky' success is a central theme of this text. However, if we are really are intimately linked to other dimensions beyond our immediate perception, is anything really spooky after all?

This is an introductory read – the Law of Interaction could fill several large volumes, but I hope that the 60 minutes or so which you spend reading this will provide you with an alternative and reinvigorating way of seeing the world and your place within it (this book has been designed to take about 60 minutes to read as I'd prefer you to spend your time *interacting* – therefore consider this to be a rapid blast of friendly energy to help get you off your sofa).

People who know me inspired and encouraged me to write this. Having lectured for several decades, I agreed with them that it was time to share my contribution with others beyond my immediate physical domain.

I have been fortunate to witness success stories from those whom I have taught to slightly reframe how they see the world and their place within it. If more people can gain something positive in their life from this book version, then it will represent spooky success for me – as you don't know me and I don't know you, yet we magically interacted and the sum was greater than the parts.

Reading a book should be similar to a cell phone charging up – it's a means to an end. And yet, so many enthusiasts read books such as this and equate that to taking action. Let me assure you that nothing compares to taking action and being productive. All famous and successful people took action — as only by interacting with the fabric of the universe can you make a greater impression on that fabric.

If demand continues to rise, then I will expand upon my ideas in more detail in a lengthier piece of work. In the meantime, I'm here to nudge you and challenge you. Remember that the boulder which destroyed the dinosaurs was probably ever so slightly nudged out of its regular orbit by another asteroid millions of years previously and so set off on an entirely different direction: it really is true that the slightest ripple can affect the direction of the mightiest wave; that applies to the large and the small, and it applies to you too, such is the nature of things.

I'm sure you're aware that the world is now awash with self-help, self-improvement and You-Can-Really-Do-It tomes. Some are quite thought-provoking. I welcome these contributions to our understanding of nature, the universe and our place within it. If one person can realise their potential through someone else's encouragement then I salute them.

I know of one individual, for example, who is worth about 50 million dollars today precisely because he read some books and attended some seminars. His life was transformed. But it was only revolutionized because he altered his mode of thinking, took persistent action and interacted with the right people.

I've spent decades in education in several countries, where every day is about giving people those little nudges and watching them go off in a new direction with a greater sense of hope and self-belief. Many other people, though, are lost within the realms of obscurity as they're hoping, for example, to maybe win the lottery one day — blissfully ignorant that they are perhaps more likely to be killed by a bolt of lightning on their way to buy a lottery ticket than they are to actually win the thing.

Society is less enriched as a consequence. These individuals are, by and large, small ripples. They do contribute to the greater fabric that connects us, but through self-imposed artificial limitations, a lack of awareness of the universal forces at work and the damage done to individuality through the socialization process, their potential lies untapped — like hard to reach oil, or gold that is located too deep underground.

Those who are waves are contributors on a much larger scale. I presume that you are interested in turning your ripple into a wave and so you find us meeting here today through the mechanism of the printed word.

Some parts of what will follow in this book may spook you a little bit (particularly in chapter 2).

Please believe me when I say that this is not my intention. Hopefully, you'll just find them to be rather eerie, but I will make occasional reference to short anecdotes for illustrative purposes to demonstrate how other forces are most definitely out there and that they sometimes — very deliberately — interact with our physical domain.

Chapter 2

Interactions from Non-Physical Levels

Note to the reader: some of the following section may perhaps spook you, so don't read alone; or skip to the next chapter if you're of a delicate composition with regard to so called supernatural activities. These personal anecdotes are little examples of real events which led me to profoundly question convention and to seek enlightenment through a greater appreciation of the Law of Interaction.

What time will the sun rise and set tomorrow? These are basic questions rooted in the natural sciences and we can go off and find definitive answers to them (by taking a so called positivist approach).

However, if I was to ask you: do ghosts exist? I've moved away from science and into philosophy. I've moved away from the comfort zone of our cosy dimensions and into the wonderful realm of supposition, belief or faith; call it what you will.

At first, such a question may appear unfathomable, but we can look at the evidence and perhaps draw some useful conclusions. For example, you seldom hear about hunter gatherer ghosts stalking people's houses. Fred Flintstone lookalikes don't seem to be too interested in forming apparitions very much these days. We could deduce then that ghosts are spirits of the deceased who have yet to fully come to terms with their new situation. Trapped between dimensions, they wander uneasily until such times as their consciousness finally (and no doubt, reluctantly) acknowledges the different realm in which it finds itself.

However, as we've already discussed, you can't connect with our fabric without influencing it. Every ripple counts. That is law. We are surrounded by energy. And this is the key point to spooky success — our journeys are touched in various ways by non-physical forces and by our own invisible thought processes — all of which contribute in tangible form to the material world.

Due to the myriad of supernatural tales which abound (almost everyone has, or at least knows somebody, who has had some spooky encounters), the journey between the physical and non-physical world doesn't really exist. In fact, in a sense, they're already in the same room, and are sitting side-by-side wherever you may go. For us, in human form, the leap between them is rendered difficult due to the nature of our physicality; however, our thoughts are not limited by such physical constraints.

I have no doubt that non-physical entities do have a bearing upon our lives – but for some people more than others, depending on how their radio is tuned (I'm speaking metaphorically here, of course).

Here's an actual radio example of an anecdote from my past experience. One time, I was woken up in the middle of the night by an alarm shrieking inside the house. I had no idea of the source of this – I didn't have such an alarm. Frantically, I scrambled around, wondering how many neighbors I would be waking up. And then I spotted it ... a shower radio, which had sat on my bathroom wall for months, had somehow been pulled off and was now resting face down in my bathroom sink with its heavy switch (at the rear) flicked over from the radio to the alarm setting. What really puzzled me is that I had absolutely no idea that this bathroom piece even had an alarm function. I switched it off and, somehow, got a little bit more sleep. The next morning, though, I found out that an aunt of mine — who had been ill for a while — had been rushed to hospital overnight as she was dying from lung cancer. Unfortunately, she did pass away several days later and I was subsequently a pallbearer at her funeral.

My interpretation of this sequence of events: I was warned that something was wrong with a family member. What I also acknowledged was how clever the non-physical force was for sending me a message through a mechanism that I hadn't even been aware of without alarming me — if I can use the pun — in my bedroom.

Messages regarding those who are tripping into different dimensions (i.e., dying) can take many forms. My mother and grandmother recalled a quiet night at home being shattered by three large thumping punches on the living room wall from an unseen force. My grandmother casually remarked that: 'Someone was on their way out.' My great grandmother died the same evening.

When my grandfather died (a World War 2 veteran), my grandmother was living with us as they had separated (divorce was a social taboo, so technically they only separated — for about 30 years). On the night of his passing, the unmistakable sound of an invisible galloping horse and carriage could be heard thundering through the bedroom during the night. She knew, again, that death was close for someone. There was no visual spectacle; only the sound of the running horse as it diligently went about its errand of collecting the soul of the deceased.

My grandmother was rather nonplussed by all of this as her mindset was a product of her life experiences in Scotland. In her youth she recalled going up the communal staircase to her family apartment. One day, she took a staircase and turned to take the next set — but her path had been blocked a headless figure sitting on large bunch of clothes and wearing a Victorian-style maid's outfit. She recalled other strange events in that particular old apartment block. One day she said it was full of World War 1 soldiers and sailors who were suddenly all assembled, sitting there quietly with their backs to the walls watching her walk by. She had no doubt that they were spirits. Back in the day, such blocks of housing only had one communal toilet. Her brother remembers going to the toilet room and witnessing the bizarre sight of a strange being standing there fully covered in feathers.

Fortune tellers are a more common route for those looking for better days or seeking answers through an interaction process with the non-physical. Some are exceptionally good. Allow me to illustrate: a friend of a close family member attended a fortune telling session that was being held by a group of friends in a residential house. It was one of those situations where the hired guest with the special powers goes into the bedroom and those who wish to participate would then go in one at a time to see her for a reading. One lady waited her turn and eventually went in to have her fortune told, but, surprisingly, she was informed that instead of a face-to-face discussion, the fortune teller would write it all down for her. She was also clearly instructed to only open the sealed envelope containing her fortune when she got home. A bit bizarre? Yes. However, the same lady in question was killed that very evening in a car crash on her way home ... when they retrieved the envelope, they found that it contained a blank sheet of paper.

I've witnessed the meanest German shepherd dog you can possibly imagine become a shivering and whimpering wreck when in the presence of a fortune teller. Animals vibrate at slightly different frequencies, so can see and hear things within these dimensions which we cannot. Something clearly spooked that dog; perhaps it was the aura from an inter-dimensional assistant that was visible to his canine eye.

Much earlier, when I was only 13 years old, I also recall a sudden voice entering the physical dimensions and breathing very slowly and loudly in my bedroom during the night. A strange glowing light accompanied the voice — it loitered in the hallway and was visible through a glass door. I shared a room with my older brother at that time. He remembers it well too. The incident actually happened twice in the same night; perhaps, the non-physical entity wanted to make their point twice, just in case there was any ambiguity. The next morning, at school, I remember sitting in the Physics class thinking: 'You really all haven't got a clue. Our understanding of conventional physics is only the tip of the iceberg and I know for sure from first-hand experience.' Yes, it was a scary experience.

At an even younger age, I remember my mother bought two wooden African dolls, each was about 10 inches in height. She was always buying ornaments and our house was cluttered with things. They had long silver earrings that were coiled around in hanging formations of various lengths. Every day I noticed that the earrings had been altered. Their shapes always looked radically different. The statues would also turn and face different ways every day. The only thing that was consistent about them was how much they changed. I thought nothing of it — someone was obviously playing about with them. One evening the topic finally came up in the family conversation – all of us were wondering who was dabbling with these earrings. When we realized that no one had been touching them, and that we had all thought that someone else had been playing about with them, we quickly got rid of the statues. The lesson was that non-physical entities can form attachments with physical objects. They can co-exist, connect and bond.

On the topic of objects, one deeply religious local man told me of a problem that a family were having with some small ornamental masks that they had bought. They were convinced that they had been a malign influence since coming into their house as wall decorations. Convinced of their view, he promptly threw them into their coal fire – and there, burning away to oblivion, the masks screamed and howled ferociously while he prodded them with a poker.

I also remember a one foot tall toy monkey that regularly altered its shape. A cousin had passed it on as she didn't like the look of it. She felt uncomfortable around it for some reason, but didn't want to throw it in the bin. Sitting on a chair on its own in one of our bedrooms, the toy chimpanzee would change its expressions. One day it would have a subtle smile, but the following day it would look angst — grimacing as if a spear had just been driven into his back. The next day it would have a neutral look, and so on.

I should have learned my lesson about objects but I recall having the notion to buy a box set of horror films once — for a while afterwards my bed was being shaken at night. The batch of DVD's was the only new thing that had come into the house at that point in time; suffice to say I got rid of them.

As a result of such experiences, I would never buy antique items. In fact, I don't even buy second-hand books or borrow library books, as I cannot be sure of their historical journey or whom they came into contact with; I'm very wary of them.

I will provide one other anecdote to illustrate this point about the physical object linking with the non-physical entity: in my student days, one Tuesday morning, I was having a long rest in bed as I had no lectures to attend that day. I stayed with my family as I studied close to home. I was in bed listening to music with headphones on and having a lazy time. In between the songs there are those 5 or ten second gaps that you get on albums, and during the pauses I could hear what I can only describe as a roaring cacophony of voices coming through from the living room area. It happened time after time between each song. I wondered who else was in and had left the TV on blaring. The noise sounded like a regular bar scene — with lots of people talking, laughing, shouting and much general ribaldry going on. A male voice in particular stood out. Eventually I got up and went through to the living room to investigate. As I did so, the noise abruptly ceased. The living room was empty. I was at home all alone. This shook me up, naturally.

Later that evening I told other family members about it. My brother immediately asked: 'Has anything new come into the house lately?' My mother said yes and mentioned that she had brought in a picture the previous night of what she referred to as the 'Black Madonna'. Along with a group of other women, she attended a small Catholic prayer group at her local church every Monday evening and they would take turns to take home the picture of the 'Black Madonna' that they used as an aid to prayer. My mother was highly skeptical of my story of the wall of noise and said that I must have been imagining things, although this was the first time that she'd agreed to take home the picture. The next evening, though, she came into my room and said: 'You're right. I heard exactly what you did when I was upstairs alone tonight.' She never availed herself of the opportunity to take the picture home again.

On a more positive note and on the issue of 'spooky' encounters with regard to health, I have an interesting tale regarding my mother and the interconnection between the physical and non-physical realms. She is firmly of the view that a Peruvian – from the Dominican Order who died in 1639 in Lima — visited her as she lay in a hospital bed in Scotland in 1970. When I was a toddler she apparently came close to death through pernicious anaemia. A Catholic priest came to visit her as she was dying — at the very young age of 27 — and well before her time. He left her a little card and a relic. It was of St. Martin de Porres, a Peruvian saint. The relic contained a small piece of white cloth that was said to have touched his bones. She didn't think much of it, but, overnight, as she lay awake in bed and all was still in the hospital ward, she said that an unexplained shadow suddenly appeared and passed directly over her. No one was walking around and the lights were all dimmed. The night nurse at the front of the ward was busy with her desk duties and the other patients were sound asleep. With immediate effect, she began to make a remarkable recovery and, to this day, many years later, she maintains a strong interest in St. Martin de Porres whom she credits for helping her to survive this near-death experience. Apparently he was an animal lover and looking after animals is a huge part of her life too. Let's put it this way: she's never had to buy a cat, but there have always been plenty of furry faces around. Incidentally, during his lifetime, this saint was said to be known for his power of bipolar location (the ability to be in two places at once). Perhaps he enjoyed his trip to Scotland many centuries later; after all, as we've already observed, space and distance are irrelevant in the world of our thoughts.

I hope none of these little spooky anecdotes have frightened you. That is not my intention. I would never dabble in occult practices and hopefully you don't either. For example, I know about houses that have been wrecked during Ouija Board games (which I didn't, and never would, participate in). I also recall one time when I woke up during the night — not in my own house but at a friend's – and watched a ghost figure — an old man, of average height, with white hair in a white shroud who was standing at the bottom of the bed. He was gazing curiously at my feet area for a while with a puzzled expression. I watched him until he suddenly noticed that I had woken up. He turned, looked at me shocked and instantly vanished.

In case, you're wondering, I did get up and go home: the thought of going back to sleep after that incident was out of the question. I can still clearly see his face to this day, including the wart on his lower left cheek. Perhaps the ability to spook each other works both ways.

Chapter 3

The Universal Fabric and You

It is apparent that we are not alone. If we could see, hear, smell, taste or feel the interactive energy forces that swirl around us, we would most certainly adopt a whole new approach to our day-to-day experience.

We all accept that a canine can hear the dog whistle that we can't – but it doesn't mean that the sound wave isn't present in the same room as you. Similarly, we are surrounded by radio waves at various frequencies. Again, we can't discern them with our physical senses, but we know with certainty that they're there. Through time, our sensory abilities can wax and wane – for example, manufacturers of alarms know that young people can hear certain sounds that older people cannot.

As well as in terms of the physical senses, perhaps children are more spiritually aware too? It is common for children to see and hear unusual things that adults in the same room cannot.

Many of us lose that link to the world of wonders as we become wrapped up in the needs and wants of our physicality and daily routine. Beyond the mystic curtain of organized religion, we are also taught by society to be more earthly — as by doing so, it's much easier to socialize you, control you and therefore manipulate your character on the anvil of conformity.

Ergo, the jump from childhood to adulthood often means the extinguishing of your dreams too. However, it appears evident that those who harness 'spooky success' are those who have a great belief in their goals and intentions. They have unswerving faith in their destinies and take decisive purposeful action within a positive mindset. Are they literally shaping their world through their thoughts and deeds? Are they tapping into unseen pools of potential realities that lie dormant until matching energy waves come along? Like practitioners of alchemy, they seem to be successful in rearranging matter according to their wishes.

Now, let me welcome you also as an important part of the interwoven fabric of time and space. In fact, without you, our dimensions would be incomplete. Like the Planet Jupiter or a distant constellation, you are also a component of the here and now. In some respects, you're much more powerful than a mighty planet or galaxy as you have a significant bearing on the immediate world around you.

Science fiction stories about time travel always caution: 'Don't interfere with the timeline.' In doing so they are acknowledging our embedded interconnectedness and the unique influence that we have upon the dimensions around us.

For example, here's a quick thought to consider: my maternal grandfather whom I referred to earlier was a survivor of the Dunkirk evacuation. This military incident took place back in June 1940 when the Nazis had the British and French armies trapped on a French beach. Around 338,000 soldiers succeeded in fleeing to fight another day. Had a single German bomb or bullet been a few degrees to the left or right during that battle, I wouldn't be here and you wouldn't be reading this today either.

Likewise, whenever I help one of my students achieve a higher grade by giving them some encouragement, or perhaps a new angle on something, then it's all due to the magnificent alignment and culmination of the tiniest of ripples that have occurred down through the ages.

Most journeys start with baggage, but paradoxically I want you to drop your baggage. I want you all alone. I want you to jettison your old thoughts. Ah, you see, that's the hard part where 99% of people fail. It sounds so simple yet to achieve it you need to swim against the tide of your subconscious programs and all of your mental subroutines to date.

Emptying your mind of the clutter that abounds in modern life is a good starting point in seeking greater success and raising your spiritual frequency. When you quieten your life, you can hear more. To use one historical example: before Jesus of Nazareth embarked on his ministry, he spent 40 days and nights in the desert. He emerged from the experience with a mission.

You too must find contemplative quiet and rest. It's no surprise that 'retreats' are a common route to thinking differently. The corporate world, for example, is well aware of the value of Away Days, or weekend conferences in different locations — as getting out of your regular environment and spending quality time in reviewing a situation from a fresh perspective can be most worthwhile.

On an individual level, prolonged respite periods can facilitate in an inner search for your purpose, destiny and real goals in life. When you hush the humdrum noise of daily routine, your mind is more likely to raise its frequency with regard to you and your place in the world.

To use an analogy: astronomers dislike streetlights as they pollute their view of the night sky. When viewed from busy urban areas, the stars can seem sparse. However, in the countryside, the pollution lifts and there they are — thousands of them in all of their majestic celestial glory. As the natural world is obscured by the pollution of daily life, so are the non-physical realms through the pollution of daily strife. One of my best ever night sky vistas took place when I was in Turkey. Having visited the ruins of the famed Temple of Artemis in Ephesus that day (one of the ancient Seven Wonders of the World), it was a profound moment. Reconnecting with the non-physical energy that surrounds you is possible if you're prepared to break free for a while and open your mind to the inspirational opportunities that abound.

Goal setting can emerge from the stillness and quiet of that void. Most people, though, have vague goals and lack faith in their manifestation. Even writing them down is a worthwhile step. Writing them down along with the first action-oriented step you're going to take to achieve them is even stronger.

It's true that successful people really do think differently. That's not a secret. Of course they do. That's how they stand out from the crowd. We can all spot a fantastic car and compare it to an old rust bucket; however, our brains and their processes are invisible to others. They're hidden from view and disguised. Thus, it's impossible to spot a successful thinker from a negative thinker, but fortunately the clues are in their deeds.

A good starting point for our journey is to ask a very fundamental question: are you really ready to embark upon a new direction in life? To do so will require some changes in your internal wiring. You're not going to remove old painful files from the hard drive of your mind; instead you're going to store them away in a separate folder. They're always a part of you. They were elements of your journey to date after all, but they're not going to influence you and they're certainly not going to hurt you. So, the broken relationship that left you in despair, the job you didn't get and the friend who let you down are all like black and white photos from the past. Look at how old they now seem. In fact, there's even a touch of quaint nostalgia to them – the old you before you discovered how to rationalize defeat and turn it into positive energy.

Let me be clear about something: regardless of inter-dimensional interventions, mental toughness is a prerequisite for success. Our immediate dimensions demand it. I won't pretend to be a Pollyanna and fool you into thinking that this a paradise location inhabited by friendly people who all want what's best for you. You know otherwise. Many self-help and motivational texts like to play around with flowery imagery. They emphasize love and bask in Edenic imagery such as waterfalls and rainbows. However, would you send a naïve traveller out along a dangerous path? Hopefully not. For example, consider the Holocaust in which 6 million people perished. In that dark chapter of human history one of the most sophisticated nations on earth effectively sentenced millions to death by means of chemical weapons purely on the grounds of their religion and ethnic group. Sadly, tales of other human atrocities could fill libraries.

It is abundantly evident that this world can be a most difficult place in which to operate. After all, anthropologically, we are the descendents of the best fighters, who were more than likely the quickest to revert to violence against other species and each other. Forget the Tyrannosaurus Rex. It would be fair to say that, in this Anthropocene epoch, our species is the most destructive, thoughtless and selfish to ever grace this planet.

People though (essentially, electrically charged bags of water with other minerals) are your contemporaries and an interaction process with them is demanded; as a result, you need to accept some degree of connectivity with a multitude of stage characters with different and competing agendas. Like mighty tectonic plates colliding, the human interaction process is where new worlds are formed and take shape. Any time you have two or more people together, you have some kind of collective development taking place and something new is being added to the overall human experience. Those little invisible sparks between us are forever lighting the candles and fires of human progress, for better or for worse.

Mental resilience and the ability to rationalize setbacks can take you a long way. Most of your fellow travellers suffer from flawed thinking and have an inability to reason properly. To break free from these settings you need to learn to be your own best friend and to pivot your mind in a positive direction whenever trouble calls (which it will, as life is designed that way). A pivot could mean reframing a setback to reduce its significance. Then finding a more positive thought and riding that wave onto the next one.

Consider the fact that people love diamonds. Diamond is a beautiful substance. It's also exceptionally hard. However, by experiencing setbacks over a vast period of time, that prolonged pummelling led to them becoming beautiful, exquisite and admired. If you're going to become a metaphorical diamond, then you must also accept challenges that — if you allow them — will character-build and enlighten you along the way. Consequently, you will emerge stronger and wiser.

Being your own best friend can go a long way to getting you into the right frame of mind. In contrast, so many of us are our own worst enemy. We beat ourselves up and have a unique propensity to wallow in the negative. Sadly, it's not a surprise then that suicide rates usually exceed murder rates.

In order to tap into spooky success, developing a positive mindset is of critical importance. This doesn't simply mean that you permit yourself the occasional feel-good session; it's much more profound than that. It means developing an embedded positive view of yourself and your place in the world. Of course, you have flaws. Everyone does, but don't beat yourself up over them. Make the most of what you have and always be your best pal. You can communicate with yourself through your own internal voice (which writers refer to as *internal discourse*). Make that voice work for you and to forever be on your side, through the good times and not so good times.

There are no more powerful thoughts than your own thoughts. That signal is the strongest that you'll ever encounter. Many of us continuously emit negative messages and slowly destroy the recipient from within; make sure you tune your signal into a positive frequency. I know that can sound difficult to do, but with time you can learn to pivot away from problems and to become much more energized and solution-orientated.

Every cloud has a silver lining — that old cliché is actually true, again as, spookily, it's designed that way — after all, in the highbrow subject of Mathematics (the science of spatial and numerical relationships), don't two negatives equal a positive?

When you see birds, for example, you're looking at the descendants of the dinosaurs. If the asteroid that wiped them out 65 million years ago had missed, they wouldn't be here today and neither would you. From unspeakable cataclysm came new hope and new opportunities; and so, on your voyage, accept that success is seldom a straight line. That's what most people are looking for; hence why they seldom break free from routine as the straight line to glory seldom exists.

Here's a little anecdote to illustrate: a friend of mine was refused entry to a bar once. He was angry, resentful, hurt and rather frustrated. Forced to alter his plans for the evening, he went to a different bar – and, spookily, he immediately met his future wife there. Whenever I see their son, I afford myself a wry smile as I witnessed the meandering process that led to his creation. In effect, a new person — a new world — was formed from the apparent chaos of the human interaction process.

Such tales are all around if you look for them. For example, had the Beatles not been rejected by Decca Records, we quite possibly would never have heard of them. They experienced failure, but through the guile and persistence of their manager, Brian Epstein, they eventually signed a record contract with EMI Records ... and the rest is cultural history.

Through some work in the music industry, I had the pleasure of a private visit inside Studio 2 at the world famous Abbey Road Studios in London. This is the actual room where the Beatles recorded most of their highly successful albums. Some of their original instruments were still there. Spookily, inside that hallowed sonic turf I felt a much deeper presence. It was a rather intangible thing, but that room felt like no ordinary music recording room to me.

As an aside, on entering Abbey Road Studios earlier that Sunday afternoon, the sound engineer who was looking after us warned us to watch out for 'the ghost'. I asked him which level of the building the spook inhabited and he confirmed that it was the level (upstairs) on which we would be remastering a few songs. Everyone laughed... However, later, as we sat squeezed onto the obligatory recording room sofa, opposite the controls, I felt what I can only describe as a fridge door being prised open. Some kind of presence then slowly passed through us. I felt the motion as it gradually eased by. I looked to the others – but they were as normal – laughing and joking. Puzzled, I asked them about the sudden rush of cold air, but no one else appeared to have been aware of anything out of the ordinary.

Regardless of your take on that little spooky encounter at Abbey Road, if you investigate the background of your favorite musicians, writers or actors, you'll probably find that two consistent things keep emerging about their journey to success: firstly, that they experienced setbacks and adversity; and secondly, that some kind of chance encounter or apparently random event helped propel them to stardom and greatness.

Such anecdotes abound; why — because, again, it's designed that way. A fly may land on a lion. He may even tickle his ear, but the lion continues to focus on the bigger picture. Likewise, if you want to leave your mark within this set of dimensions then you will also need to become a lion and ignore the flies that come your way. They will surely land on you: from the broken down car and the burst water pipe, to the unexpected deluge of rainfall when you're out in the open; but by keeping faith in your overall purpose and greater sense of perspective, you will to continue on your path to success.

As well as gradually raising your awareness of the role of invisible forces in shaping current events, feeling good in the moment is also vital to a positive mindset for taking action and seeking success. After all, as they say, there's no time like the present. The word vital suggests vitality — being energized, confident and positive. So, indulge yourself from time to time. You know what you like the most, so go for it and enjoy it. Why do you think you are in physical form? To experience. To learn, grow and avail yourself of rewards during your journey. Enjoy the bar of chocolate, or the drink, or the walk with the dog as feeling good will also release the chemicals that will keep you more youthful. Indeed, you were the product of a temporary sexual energy: Energy + Action = Creation. Congratulations, that's how you arrived here. Flushing out stress is like clearing out the unwelcome limescale from water pipes. Some degree of indulgence will keep you youthful and young at heart. After all, you've earned it, but remember that Nature is your tutor in this regard. Consider the earth's distance from the sun. It's finely balanced: if you get too near fire, you burn, but if you're too far away, you freeze. The lesson is that moderation and a wise degree of balance will lead to a longer and more pleasant journey.

Nature is your reference point and instructor in many respects. The earth's surface is littered with brutal asteroid and meteorite impacts, but we can't see most of them as they're covered up (unlike the barren moon). You too, will carry some invisible scars as you make progress in life. These are actually signs of progress and such setbacks will enhance your chances of success if you can learn from them.

So, if your interactions are based upon whom or what you connect with on your journey, do you have more in common with a galaxy billions of miles away or a supernatural entity in your living room? On the one hand, you and that galaxy — despite the distance — exist in the same set of dimensions within our physical domain; but on the other hand, the supernatural entity is close to you, and is an intelligent design who is perhaps interested in your experience. The answer will depend upon your framing and perception of how you fit into these dimensions of time and space. The vast majority of people would dismiss the distant galaxy as being too far away to be of any consequence to their everyday experience and would dismiss the supernatural entity as not existing in the first place. However, I suspect that you know differently. Due to the speed of light, the entity is of more consequence — simply because it is not bound by the physical constraints of the here and now. Is that of significance?

Yes, because the human experience is based on interactions with all things – be it other people, forces of nature or the invisible – such as subconscious connections.

Here's an example to illustrate that unseen connectivity: one night I had a dream that I was in Wellington, New Zealand. I'd never been to New Zealand or even knew of anyone who'd been there for a visit. And yet, it was a very vivid dream. I could see buildings. I was strolling about in the daytime and I had an acute sense of being there. It was one of those dreams that you actually remember when you wake up in the morning and go about your day. I thought nothing of it and fired up the computer to check my emails. When I did so, there was a surprise message waiting for me at the very top of the pile from someone I hadn't seen in a very long time. It went along the lines of: *'Hi, John. It's Sarah Jane, one of your ex-students. I'm taking a year out to travel the world. I'm currently in Wellington, New Zealand! I just thought I'd drop you a quick line to say hello ...'*

A random event? A spooky coincidental experience? No.

Two things can be drawn from this incident. Firstly, through our thoughts we are connected at a subconscious level. When I was asleep I was more in tune and receptive to this process. Note the use of the word receptive, to use a simile – it's like a radio mast.

Secondly, a study of the antipodes (diametrically opposite points on the earth's surface) shows that Scotland and New Zealand are as far apart as is physically possible. I was in Scotland and she was in New Zealand. Theoretically, if you started digging a hole in Scotland, you would eventually emerge off the coast of New Zealand – meaning that the two geographical locations are effectively poles apart. Yet our thoughts had traversed this distance as if we were next door to each other.

So, at the subconscious level, distance is clearly irrelevant. Invisible forces are much more powerful than physical distances. They don't concern themselves with such trivialities. Do you mind if I indulge myself with some hyperbole and repeat that with some exclamation marks? The invisible are more powerful than physical distances! They don't concern themselves with such trivialities!

I also remember being jolting out of bed one morning for no apparent reason. Something had spooked me and I immediately got up. Nothing seemed unusual. I noted the time on the bedside clock; the red digits cutting through the darkness of the late winter's morning. The house was still and I couldn't even remember dreaming about anything; yet, I was somehow compelled to get up right away. I thought nothing of the strange incident and went about my day as normal. The news was dominated by the tragic tsunami disaster that had been unfolding in Japan. They announced the time that the wave first struck. I didn't click. Then one news bulletin mentioned the UK time that the tsunami had reached the shore of Japan — to the minute, it was the exact same time that I'd been jolted out of bed six thousand miles away on the other side of the world.

Another random event? Another spooky coincidental experience? No.

I concluded, once again, that we are interconnected at a deeper level — even with regard to total strangers. I've never been to Japan or conversed much with a Japanese person. I have absolutely no connections to the country and yet my brain had picked up on something: an interconnectedness that transcends known friends or relations, and an interconnectedness which hints that, spookily, we are linked through much higher energy patterns to lots of other fellow companions in time and space.

Such experiences could therefore be taken to yet another level. If distance means nothing at the subconscious level, then does it transcend Planet Earth? Are we connected to the entire universe and therefore influenced at a subtle level beyond our wildest imagination? Reframed, we're asking if our thoughts can cut through gravity. The answer is obviously: Why not? The impact of such intergalactic interconnection is perhaps more difficult to quantify as we may find it hard to recognize them.

When we're inspired, we're in spirit. In spirit with what? Perhaps with other entities, or perhaps to a state of consciousness of which we are also a part. Great music, writing and scientific innovations often involve tapping into an ocean of infinite possibilities: a boundary-less place, where the only limitations are the ones we are prepared to accept.

However, there's a process which has been developed to build barriers between you and the less recognizable forms of energy that abound. It's an all-pervasive process. It's invisible; yet it's very powerful. It starts with the best of intentions immediately after your birth and it pretends to be your friend. Its influence is so embedded into you that it renders most self-help strategies to be futile uphill battles.

Its name? —The socialization process …

Chapter 4

Socialization and Your Escape Velocity

Faith and belief in your own abilities are anchored in your thought processes. Being the social animal that you are, these signals are often turned down – like a volume switch being set to a low level. By doing so, you are also detaching yourself from successfully tuning into other forces that are less obvious.

By interaction and through the process known as socialization 'they' reduced your wave to a ripple. 'They' are often authority figures, be it parents, schoolteachers and even your peer group (whose value systems you will adopt).

It is said that with age comes experience and hopefully some wisdom too. When you're 10 years old, another year is adding 10% onto your life experience. When you're 50, another year is only adding 2% to your life experience. Small wonder then that many comment on how the years seem to accelerate as they age — as it's all due to perception. That perception, though, is usually also one of increasingly entrenched views and damaging limiting beliefs.

Those near death often speak very candidly and lament that their biggest regret was not being themselves more. Nearing the exit point from their current physical state, they correctly pinpoint the damage done by the invisible ropes of the socialization process and how the constant barrage of social conditioning extinguished their chutzpah.

When I was around 6 years old and at primary school, the teacher asked us what we wanted to be when we grew up. Straight away, I put my hand up and replied without hesitation: 'A spaceman.'

The interesting thing is that no one laughed. My classmates nodded in approval and took it seriously. Why not an astronaut? The world was our proverbial oyster and we could do whatever we wanted. In contrast, no high school pupil would be likely to offer such a response without fear of ridicule in the school corridors later. Because by then, they've got us ... they've knocked the dreams out of us, made us conform and put us into a very restrictive box. Being social animals we're designed to fit in. Banishment was man's greatest fear – why do you think Adam and Eve were said to have been kicked out of the Garden of Eden? The classic tale informs us to be wary. The message is clear: if you don't toe the line regarding the rules, you're out the door.

In our Digital Era, social media has served to reinforce the primitive pack mentality. Instead of liberating us and promoting individuality, technology has enslaved us, and there's an even greater pressure now to go with the flow as the scope for ridicule and a public lampooning is only a mouse click away.

Sociologists tell us that our perceptions and everyday experiences are shaped and moulded by a vast range of factors. Would Hitler have been a charity worker had his interactions and experiences been different? Proponents of free will and human autonomy still acknowledge that we are the product of our life experiences and influences. These micro interactions combine and are manifest in our collective consciousness. The Nazis are prime examples of how the collective brain of a society — of perhaps the most civilized country in the world at that time — could be altered and sent down a different and destructive path. If people are ripples and waves, then like all ripples and waves, a critical mass can be reached where a new path will be charted.

Every day we are obliged to conform. Like rain hitting a rock, that relentless process will gradually, but indelibly, leave its mark. It will slowly condition you. Unfortunately, it will also probably destroy your dreams and make you settle for second best. You'll underperform and will therefore be highly unlikely to achieve your potential.

Consider a comparison from the natural world: to escape gravity, a rocket needs to travel at around 25,000 miles per hour. This is known as the earth's escape velocity. What escape velocity will you need to reach to throw off the limiting beliefs imposed on you through the powerful socialization process?

Very few of us escape the trap of socialization. To be a success, you will need to rediscover your inner child again. Fresh in the physical dimensions, you were a much bolder piece of work – as where you came from did not wallow in such pesky limitations. It took a bit of time, but they got you.

I remember the school headmistress once pulled me up for smiling in a corridor. She even made me report to her office for the alleged offence ... and we wonder why the joy of youth fades away. Her real problem was that I had refused to take part in several activities such as a school play (frankly, because I couldn't be bothered). This was an early lesson for me in the political interplay between individuals and the dark art of authority.

Interestingly, when we dream we re-enter a more natural state with regard to the power of our thoughts and the manifold signals that bombard us from energy patterns. Fortunately, the threshold of the dream state is also the border post for the socialization process.

There, our radio antenna is finally allowed to wander and explore other frequencies.

Throwing off the shackles of social conditioning is therefore key to your journey to success. Meditate in a manner that works for you and discard all of the artificial elements they taught you: even your name, for example, is not really your name. Somebody else just made it up. Neither is it the year that they taught you it is. In fact, whatever year you think you're currently living in, it's anything but that year. The calendar is an artificial construct hallmarked by the arrogance of the prevailing culture that invented it. Maybe it's really about the year 4.5 billion — as that's the age of Planet Earth; or maybe it's 13.7 billion as that's approximately the amount of time our physical domain has been on the go.

In fact, you're not living on Planet Earth either — again, that's an artificial handle. Your planet's name is a misnomer as, due to its surface composition, it should really be called Planet Water, but again, human arrogance won the argument on that one.

Through reframing your perceptions, try to gradually shake off the baggage of such routine trappings and see things differently. Breaking free from the bonds of socialization will significantly enhance your ability to think differently and to rationalize the world around you.

If you're afraid to take that first step to achieving your desires due to a fear of how you'll be perceived, then I'm afraid to say that unfortunately 'they' have got you on a leash. They effectively control you. You're their little plaything. Like obedient dogs tethered outside grocery stores awaiting the return of our masters, the majority of us are bound by the views of others.

Symbolic interactionists would note that our personalities are formed, like reflections, through our interactions with others – hence, the trauma of solitary confinement where the real loss is the taking away of one's identity. How sad that so much ambition and creative endeavour is smothered in the cradle due to the artificial limitations imposed by others. Curiously, your lack of success will make them feel good – hence, the underlying root motivation in boxing you in. Your achievements will highlight their lack of achievements. It goes back to that fear of banishment and being ostracized. Again, it's rooted in flawed thinking. Overcome your own negative thinking and others will follow you.

Taking action to remedy this through belief and visualization is sometimes only a step away. For example, staying on the subject of my schooldays and formative years, I remember that I was awful at football (soccer). In those puerile social circles, that was a particularly uncool attribute to have. Nevertheless, I pressed on and regularly played the game despite sometimes being the last guy to be picked for teams (usually because no one else was available). Despite my limited ability, I remember one night deciding that I would score a 40 yard goal in the next game. That was it. I just made a decision that I would do it. Sure enough, during the next game, I charged up the pitch, spotted a space and fired off an unstoppable shot that sailed into the roof of the net. The others looked on perplexed — it was obviously a fluke. However, I decided that it wasn't. Again, the night before the next school football game, I decided that I would hammer in another long range spectacular – and again, I did. The ball soared into the net with power and precision leaving the goalkeeper no chance. My teammates and the opposition were left bewildered.

These goals (literal goals in this case) happened simply because I had decided that they would. That was it. Sports psychologists would confirm the merits of imagining success and then watching it unfold.

The lesson here is that we are more powerful than we assume we are and certainly more powerful than others assume us to be. In a similar vein, medical placebos can work simply because the recipient has decided that they will.

You've heard it said that a little bit of positive thinking can go a long way. There's an industry built around this principle and I certainly believe it to be true. For example, I remember failing my driving test twice. After the second ignominious attempt, I sat slumped on the sofa wallowing in my underachievement. Driving just wasn't for me ... it wasn't meant to be ... a 3rd failure would be even more embarrassing ... particularly for a guy in this gendered society ... You can see where I was mentally. I vividly recall, however, the slight shift in my thinking – I reached for that 'pivot' moment I mentioned earlier. Like a ray of sunshine coming through an overcast day, I remember thinking: 'I'm going to sit this test again and I'm going to pass it.' I rushed around to the post office and sent away for another test. I received a quick examination date, due to a cancellation, and proceeded to pass it at the 3rd attempt.

What struck me was the discernible pivot moment of shifting my thinking from bathing in the negative to becoming energized, focussed and positive. I accepted my two earlier failings but I looked forward and not backwards.

On a larger scale, but using the same principles, history is full of military generals and inventors who refused to accept defeat. They saw a route to success — however slim — and through sheer willpower and drive they got there. Like a spooky force of nature, they swept aside all before them. If you can harness positive belief and get momentum behind you, you will also be unstoppable.

If the self-help industry encourages some people to rediscover their bold inner child, think positively and achieve success then that can only be a good thing. If 10,000 people read a motivational text, 500 may actually make changes and break free (to varying extents) from their predominant mindset. 100 of them may achieve something tangible from their actions. So, I am in favor of the self-help industry, but I would draw caution to that catch-all caveat emptor that if you don't succeed then it's because you have limiting beliefs. I would point more to the deficit in reaching the escape velocity of breaking free from the bonds of your socialization process.

Unless you can do so, it will be like trying to drive a car with the handbrake still up. You'll be a pale shadow of what you could be as you'll be much more interested in conformity and approval, rather than in making progress and taking risks. You may find solace in taking incremental steps, but such small measures betray your true potential and are a path to mediocrity.

Earlier I mentioned the need to break free from your usual environment in order to re-evaluate and tap into spooky success. But for many, a sudden life changing moment — such as a near-death experience — is sometimes the trigger behind a new mindset. Do you really want to wait for that potentially fatal event before you take action? You might be 85 years of age and playing Pass the Parcel in an Old Folk's home when it finally does occur.

Those who succeed in taking positive action towards success will do so at any point in their lives, but they must be mentally in tune to hear the message. I've heard it said that you need to get lucky to be successful. On the one hand, there is some merit in this point as good fortune is always welcome, but as we have seen — through our interconnected fabric — we are the product of the interaction process, seen and unseen. Others will counter that luck is where opportunity meets preparation. It's also a manifestation of where your unseen radio antenna is proactive in drawing the circumstances to it through the invisible forces that permeate all of space and time.

It's not the case that everyone is going to be a millionaire or find the magic antidote for a dreaded disease. So, it's time to be brutally frank: some people are not hugely talented in a commercial sense; although I do believe that everyone is uniquely talented. There's nothing wrong with that; everyone still has a worthwhile role to play within the fabric.

The ripples of some individuals will be smaller than the waves of others as there is an unequal distribution of natural talent. Trust me, if you needed a heart operation or brain surgery and were wholly dependent upon me to mend you, I would certainly kill you – simply because I'm not good enough to perform those particular tasks. Let's face it: most of us will never be good enough to play for the New York Giants, or the Boston Red Sox, or Manchester United. However, you and I do have tangible talents and abilities, and we should be seeking to maximize these in order to make a positive contribution to the rich tapestry that is society.

By doing so, in whatever way, you may also be rewarded through riches. Of course, materialism and personal gain may not be your driving force. Ghandi noted that the best way to find yourself was in the service of others. What a wonderful point of view. The goals of the individual and the collective can comfortably sit simultaneously.

Conversely – but similarly (if you think about it) – the father of liberal economics, 18th century Scottish university lecturer, Adam Smith, highlighted self-interest as the unseen oil that lubricates the market economy. He gave this ubiquitous motivational driver the spooky title of the 'invisible hand'. Following his logic, if you are part of an interconnected fabric, then you will experience self-advancement only by taking others along with you. The public may enjoy the new song you write, the new recipe you make, or the new clothes that you design, but without taking others with you, you're unlikely to experience a modicum of success. Such a notion recognizes that you are an individual, but also part of a much bigger interconnected configuration called society. Your wellbeing is therefore inextricably linked with that of others.

Some sociologists would point to Gini coefficients as having a role in explaining crime levels in society — this is where greater levels of inequality in a society, tend to lead to more criminal behavior. If others are left behind, they may have more to lose. This is not a Communist war cry — far from it. It's an acknowledgement that we are interconnected at obvious — and much less obvious — levels. Why do you think so many successful people enjoy philanthropy and the giving back of some of their energy in the form of financial assistance? They're certainly not Marxists, but they're aware of something at a much more profound level.

When I look out of my kitchen window, for example, I can see an old library building (now a business development and conference center) that was funded by the legendary, Scots-American steel magnate, Andrew Carnegie. He recognized that we all have a duty to share and to give something back to benefit the overall fabric of society — in this case, through public infrastructure to encourage education. After all, education is not about 1 + 1 = 2. Instead, education is about the empowerment of others: 1+ 1 = 100.

The lesson is: apply your accrued knowledge and skills to the betterment of yourself and society. Success can therefore be found in the synergy of matching your goals and dreams with the needs, wants and desires of others. Groups can achieve more than individuals as, spookily, the sum is usually greater than the parts. This symbiotic relationship is at the core of any business idea or public service endeavour.

Remember that, through natural laws, you can be very easily influenced at a deeper and more profound level and will rearrange your world accordingly — for better or for worse.

Here's a little anecdote to illustrate: one evening after work I received an email from a friend who owns an apartment in the same block in which I also live. He was in Croatia on holiday, but his current tenant had been complaining about water leaking down from the flat above her. I looked into it and spoke to the tenant's upstairs neighbor about the issue. Those of you familiar with the law of attraction (and there's a multitude out there on it – this is not another book about it) might well guess what happened next. That very same night, after dealing with someone's leaking pipe, my own hot water tank also suddenly sprung a leak.

Fortunately, I woke a bit earlier than normal that day and so only a small puddle had appeared overnight (isn't it great to slightly beat the alarm clock and feel in control of our own destiny?).

Like corks on an ocean, we really can be easily pulled in so many different directions by the prevailing conditions, dominant forces and energy currents that surround us. Those energy currents include the predominant value systems of the people whom you hang out with. There's an old saying about choosing your friends carefully, such is the compelling influence that we can have on each other. To illustrate: yawn when amongst a small group of people and watch what quickly happens.

In contrast, those who harness spooky success are usually the strong-willed. They are the controllers, rather than the controlled.

They are the conductor and not the orchestra. This mode of thinking is probably best summed up by Winston Churchill, who once said: 'History will be kind to me for I intend to write it.'

In a nutshell, that's the essence of successful thinking and that's the *modus operandi* of that small percentage of the population who have complete faith in their talents, abilities and sense of destiny. Remember also that Churchill is still recognized in opinion polls as Britain's greatest leader; yet his route to success was anything but a straight line.

Chapter 5

From Positive Ripples to Positive Waves

At a more profound level, maybe the non-physical world looks on in horror at how we treat each other and the animal kingdom in the name of greed, gold and glory. Man really is a deeply-flawed creature. When we look at children and shake our heads at their behavior and short-termism, the spirits must do the same with us. In the nuclear age, the stakes are even higher. Man is at a critical junction in evolution: where he has the physical ability to destroy life on the planet, yet doubts persist about whether or not he has the mental capacity to deal with such technology. Like a child playing with matches under the bed, we really do need adult guidance and I've little doubt that we regularly receive this in the form of timely interventions.

As those who are inspired connect with a higher level of consciousness in another realm, then maybe non-physical entities who dwell there feel a sense of responsibility for where our technological developments have since taken us — to the potential cusp of oblivion.

My point is that the physical and non-physical coexist at the same time and that such interconnections influence our world. The non-physical can appear to dimension jump; but, by the same token, we can also connect with them through various mechanisms — gateways or portals — to the other dimensions that are around us. Indeed, prayer is a mainstream and universally-recognized method for liaison with the non-physical world and few doubt its sincerity.

I'm not a religious person, but I'd like to think that I'm a spiritual person with an awareness of the bigger picture. I believe you are too and that's why you're reading this.

I mentioned that society has a collective consciousness — a common brain, if you like, to which we contribute and feed off. What a wonderful thought: today you can change the world and the fabric that covers us all like a thin blanket as we interconnect. That being the case, why don't you use this autonomy to push our collective experience into a more positive place? If you don't think you're powerful enough to do that, then think again. Individuals create the world around us. The micro world moulds the macro world. So, take a minute to knock on your elderly neighbor's door to ask how she is. Pick up that item of litter that someone else dropped. Send somebody a 'Thank You' card. Like a torpedo of hope, small deeds send out a message to the world: we are connected and as one. Positivity is infectious.

The world is the product of interaction at the micro level i.e., you; so use that power wisely. Just as snowflakes become avalanches, ripples can become waves. Governments know this. That's why they'll design a tax system accordingly — right down to the incentives at the individual level. Why do you think, for example, that the government is keen for you to invest in buying a house? They know that you'll be plunged into debt and will work harder for several decades to pay off the mortgage — and in doing so overall national productivity will rise. One person with a mortgage won't affect a society too much, but tens of millions of them surely will. They know that you're more likely to work harder and generally keep busy when carrying a mortgage — thus having a stake in society and also being less likely to turn to crime.

The small things matter a lot — through the wonder of our interconnectedness — but, unfortunately, negativity can be insidious and infectious too. Even innocuous litter, for example, can trigger a higher murder rate in a society. Why? Because it sends out a powerful subconscious signal — i.e., that no one cares around this neighborhood and you can do what you want... Therefore, litter is a subtle green light for graffiti and a general spiral into higher-level crime. Sociologists and criminologists have known this for a long time.

You may make use of small positive steps, of course, for personal gain too. And why not? A good starting point is to rationalize what you mean by success. Many talk, for instance, of the magic figure of a million dollars or a million pounds. If you think that way of any item, you're very unlikely to ever own a million of them. Remember that a million is only one thousand thousand. In the bigger picture, it's not a lot of money.

Focussing more on adding a product or service which others may enjoy or benefit from is much more likely to lead you to material gain. In that case, ten million dollars, pounds or euros is a more realistic figure to think about. To achieve that, you'll need to build your oil rig. I'm speaking metaphorically here, but hopefully you get my point: build something that will last for a while and generate income even when you're in bed sleeping and connecting at a higher level with the world at large.

A note of caution: by taking action, your ripple in the fabric will quite possibly upset some people; after all, you've rearranged the universe — their universe too. They might seek to denigrate you, or perhaps they will see you as a threat. Jesus Christ and Adolf Hitler lived lives that were poles apart in terms of their actions and values — however, they both had something in common – they both spent time in the jail. They both got in the face of the authorities; the old cliché that turkeys don't vote for Christmas means that those with power will quite often be prepared to use it if they perceive someone or something as a threat. That could mean a business rival who doesn't welcome your competition; or perhaps you want to enter the gladiatorial arena of politics where *ad hominem* (i.e., personal) attacks should be expected as commonplace.

Whatever positive action you choose to take, remember that life is an interactive contact sport. If our entire physical system is an artificial construct created in order to experience challenges and to grow, then you should see life as being a kind of virtual reality game and you're a character in it. All's well that ends well: so, in a sense you're untouchable, as, simultaneously, you also inhabit other dimensions through your spooky interconnectedness with the non-physical.

There are so many books out there on how to think differently, set goals and work towards success (in fact, if you embarked upon reading a fraction of them, you'd probably never have the time to actually build your proverbial oil rig). Make use of the ones that work for you (read many reviews first). I do know of people who have benefitted greatly from the vast range of self-help genre materials that are out there. However, I also know of many who haven't. Perhaps they didn't shake off those limiting beliefs, or eradicate those negative sub programs after all, and were therefore doomed from the start. They didn't appreciate the Law of Interaction or achieve that necessary escape velocity in their own mind, and so remained enslaved to the chains of socialization.

Inspiration for success can be found in an abundance of sources. Even music is a sonic drug (it can alter your mental state, after all). Eureka moments are there if you're open to receiving them. Every moment is pregnant with potential. Even an empty room is anything but empty. It's crawling with life at a micro level; you just can't see it. These mini-creatures have a consciousness too and a role to play within our physical system. They must, as every atom has a purpose, is part of the great fabric and contributes in some form. Similarly, with regard to non-physical entities, there are many more of them than there are us; so without spooking you too much, it might be fair to say that it's unlikely you are alone after all, but don't be afraid as you have no reason to be.

History is full of inspiring tales of so called divine interventions. It's also full of negative stories. The yin and yang can work both ways. If you're aware of how spooky factors can influence one's life direction and possible success, then you can also rationalize that we are not quite alone in the here and now and that we are only one part of a much larger fabric.

Even if you do not believe in spirits, ghosts, angels, God, or any other myriad of energy forms inhabiting dimensions that overlap with ours, the point is that many people do. They take action accordingly (often unknowingly) and due to the interconnected fabric in which we all operate, that influence has a bearing upon you and society.

The basic mechanics of the Law of Interaction should therefore be considered by means of three key interlocking features:

- You are the interactive product of your upbringing, social environment and circumstances. As a result, through the compromising power of socialization, the real you is locked away inside your personality and, in most cases, has not been given permission to flourish. A failure to reconnect with that

purer, original, energy-form version of you is an underlying root cause behind your unrealized potential
- You are intimately connected to a much bigger fabric and so (unbeknownst to most people) your world and day-to-day experiences are continually subject to a barrage of interactive influences from both the physical and non-physical domains
- Until you understand these interactive influences and seek to harness and account for them, you will be always be a member of the orchestra of energy - rather than the conductor of the orchestra of energy (metaphorically speaking)

Use that knowledge wisely and be more open to the little nudges that come your way. They're there every single day; you just need to adjust your signal and tune into them. When you dream, for example, your inner child gets out to play again. Listen closely to the counsel of that inner child as he or she is much closer to the great universal truth than you are.

Success is not an accident; neither is it predicated on luck. Those who are more in tune with the broader range of forces that shape and influence our world are also those who have an awareness and perception of how to make interconnectivity work for them.

We are bombarded every day by unseen signals. They're all around us. Some are very obvious; some much less so; and, yes, some are downright spooky.

Chapter 6

In Summary: The Quickie Action Plan

In brief summary, I would therefore recommend that you consider the following plan of action:

- Plan some kind of retreat to reignite your spiritual connection. This doesn't mean hiding out in the desert, but it does mean stepping out of your comfort zone for a while, preferably alone in the first instance. You may need to repeat this step until you can discern that tangible changes and gradual shifts are beginning to take place in your mindset. Until you feel these changes taking place, you're only going through the motions. Throwing off the shackles of daily strife and normal routines is no mean feat. It requires patience and a dedicated quest for your inner truthful self. Like building a house, the foundation is often the hardest part. Take time to explore your inner self and find out what your values really are. History is full of sudden epiphanies and critical junctions in people's lives that led them onto new outlooks, new directions and new courses of action — usually due to unfortunate circumstances and situations that were forced upon them; however, you are probably undertaking this inner search from a relative position of comfort and stability, so the process will perhaps take longer to work through into your predominant mindset.

- Use that time for deep contemplation to examine who you really are. Recall the boldness of your childhood and question how you would like to contribute to the broader connective fabric and to your dimensions. To find out who you really are, you'll need to break free from the bonds of socialization. This will take time and may require finding a form of meditation that particularly works for you. To begin with, this may take the form of straightforward mental exercises: perhaps you'll imagine yourself at the summit of Mount Everest, or at the bottom of the Krubera Cave (the deepest in the world) or simply sitting at the window of a tranquil space station millions of miles away looking down at the dot of light that is Planet Earth. Perhaps hydrotherapy will work for you (consider how many good ideas come to people under the shower). Through trial and error, explore what works for you in this regard (ensuring, of course, that it is a safe and appropriate time and place to engage in this activity). You'll instinctively know when you feel more liberated, at rest and in tune with the energy patterns that are around you. In doing so, through reverse sociology, you'll be able to peel off the layers that engulf you and recapture your real identity. After all, as mentioned earlier, your name is not your real name. It's not the year 20-(insert the alleged current year); but you are moving at thousands of miles per hour around a ball of fire and you are more powerful than they've taught you to be. You are also deeply connected to other dimensions beyond your understanding of the current paradigms. Liberating yourself from socialization does not mean completely reinventing yourself. You will still maintain the positive aspects of the socialization process, such as your sensibilities, manners and awareness of cultural norms; but you will shake off the negative aspects of socialization, such as your limiting beliefs and the oppression of your natural — more spiritually aware — state.

- Standard motivational and life-coaching material has great merit when applied in a positive manner, so do ascertain your goals, write them down and include the first step you can take in working towards achieving them.

- Study those whose success you would like to emulate. Read up on them. Get to know them as if you're a close relative. Continue with your spiritual quest too and feed your appetite for knowledge.

- Take action. The world may indeed come to you but the word *interaction* suggests a two-way process and that means persistent commitment and good faith on your part. If the Big Bang had just stayed in its cosmic bunker, you wouldn't be reading this. Likewise, instead of living in the shadow of their potential, Christopher Columbus boldly took to the seas and the Wright Brothers bravely took to the skies.

- Note that if the first two points work really work, you'll instinctively know what to do next as you'll have tapped into the driving force and grand metaphysical turbo engine that will drive you towards spooky success. When you are following your heart's desire, you will feel self-actualized. This will mean that everyday activities such as eating and going to bed may suddenly feel like a chore — as you'll be so enthused in engaging with your true goals and desires in life. Achieving self-actualization is the real goal in spooky success. Few people attain it, mainly because they don't know what it is, or they don't believe that it's truly obtainable, or —like a fly in amber — they are trapped in the limiting beliefs imposed by others. Only you know what it is. It is your mission to probe your subconscious mind to find out what it uniquely means to you, because when you do so your heart will be on fire with zeal and the unseen energies that lurk throughout the cosmos will be happy to surf that interconnect with you.

- Many say that the universe will move when you do. If it doesn't then keep repeating these steps until that connection is established. On your journey, remember that success is seldom linear or obvious. It is often disguised and can manifest in unexpected ways. Through trial and error, find out how you can unlock the trap of socialization and reconnect with the infinite energy forms that are surrounding you every day. You'll know when you've tapped into this field, as when you do so you'll shift from glacial speed to rocket speed.

Chapter 7

Finally, Some Wise Words from an Old Bear

I will leave you now to ponder our brief meeting and to think about your next contributions to the great fabric of life. I appreciate that you have much work to do and, as mentioned in the Preface and Introduction, your valuable time would be much better spent in action-orientation.

Finally, as we part, and on a lighter note, you may wish to heed the wise old bear, Furry O'Mara, in the young adult fiction novel, *The Bear in a Safari Hat*, who counselled his nephew as the two bears took a pleasant afternoon stroll through the lush countryside (after all, your inner child would readily embrace such a scenario).

His advice in this excerpt is worth bearing in mind as you now move forward in the expectation of a better and more fulfilling future:

> *'Well, everything I learned was based on getting my paws dirty, but if you're asking, here's a few of my tips – work hard, build a good team and stay away from negative bears as they'll put the pawbrake on you. Listen to your workers, assume nothing and, above all, don't throw bazookas at blades of grass - that is to say, make your time and energy count, son. Channel it properly and don't major in minor things.'*

The two relations continued to lead the line of bears and ambled side by side.

'And another thing,' continued Furry as he narrowed his eyes in the strong sunlight and admired his native land in full bloom, 'believe in your dreams. The most wondrous sight on this planet is when the wheels of an aircraft leave the ground. Now that's a truly magical moment: a triumph of spirit and a mastery of the mind. It was all down to bears who believed it could be done. The majority, with their limiting beliefs, dismissed them as cranks but the dreamers prevailed in the end.

'You must also pursue your dreams, youngster, and never let another bear tell you otherwise. So think big, set goals and don't be afraid of failure. Remember that you learn more from defeat than victory. From the chaos of boulders and dust, mighty planets are eventually formed. Likewise, the bear who keeps trying is the bear who will finally succeed.'

'Thanks, uncle.' Brosnan appreciated more than ever before that his relative, although a rustic and hard working honey farmer, was, like most Irish bears that he had met, also a philosopher at heart.

'Never underestimate the power of positive thinking either, Brosnan Bear, and always be grateful for what you already have. When you *get up in the morning, don't think "I'm the oldest I've ever been". Instead, remind yourself that you've never been so experienced but at the same time you're the youngest that you're ever going to be.*

'A word of caution, though: remember that this planet spins on a tilted axis. It's not a meritocracy. There's corruption, ego, avarice and all sorts of shenanigans going on out there to contend with. The more you step out of your comfort zone, the more of these characters you will probably meet.

'Whoever said that there's a thin line between success and failure was telling a lie. In truth, it's a wafer thin line that separates success and failure, and most of us traverse that invisible trapeze throughout our entire lives.'

The bear in a safari hat smiled and a rabbit sprinted past without a glance.

'The world is just one big playground, youngster, and remember, like any good playground, it must contain some obstacles. They are there to challenge you so that you will learn and grow.

'Think of a diamond: it looks beautiful as well as strong and brilliant; but to get to that stage it had to go through a long and difficult journey. You will also achieve greater strength through experiencing adversity. If you ever go through a tough phase, and you will, then remember that

life is just an opera: as one Act ends, so another Act must naturally begin. For better or for worse, that is the way of things.

'Also, don't let any bear tell you that money isn't important in this world. It's usually very rich bears and very poor bears that say that. The rest of us – that big rump in the middle – need to work our hides off to get by. The money in your pocket represents the doves of financial freedom; like it or not. That's where your next mug of honey tea is coming from. Get used to that fact. Having said that, never get too hung up about money either. Remember that the so-called magical figure of a million, for example, is only a thousand thousand. It's not a lot. It's buttons really in the grand scheme of things.

'So, no matter what may happen, keep your pride and dignity, son. Never be anybody's doormat. It is better to stand on poor paws than to bend on rich knees. And remember,' added Furry with a serious frown, 'beware of the little ones.'

'You mean cubs?'

'No, the opposite! Beware of adults with little minds. You'll know them when you meet them, youngster. They want to live in a small planet. They gossip and meddle. They're naïve. They never see the bigger picture in life: be it at work, at home, in local affairs, or in world affairs, and if you ask me these bears are downright

dangerous. They'll try to pull you down to their level. They choose to see the world only through the narrow lens of the end of their nose.'

'I see.'

'One last point: don't forget to enjoy yourself. After all, that's the meaning of life. Your life is but a grain of sand on the beach of time, Brosnan Bear, so remember to let your fur down on a regular basis. The only thing that really matters is how many meads you're going to have at the weekend.

'Every bear is different so find your buttons, youngster, and when you find them enjoy pressing them because you're as unique as a tiny snowflake, or a pawprint, or a massive solar system, or a galaxy. So do what you enjoy. Self-motivation is the silent force that powers the soul. It gets a bear going,' he enthused, 'and it has to come from within to be meaningful. Also, never think that you're bigger than the universal laws of Mother Nature. If you ever start thinking that then just pick up a rock and marvel at how ancient this dear planet of ours really is.'

Farewell and flourish.

John Gold

Book 2 in the Series Now Available

"The Spooky Millionaire" by John Gold

To Contact the Author:

Email: spookysuccess@outlook.com

Printed in Great Britain
by Amazon